초등 필수 영단어 완벽

KB175735

가장 쉬운

초등영단어

따라쓰기

하루 한장의 기적

동양북스 콘텐츠기획팀 지음

📖 동양북스

나의 꿈, 나의 계획

나는 _____ 한

_____ (이)가 될 거예요.

건강 목표

생활 목표

공부 목표

목차

LEVEL 3 — 108

이 책은 이렇게 쓰세요

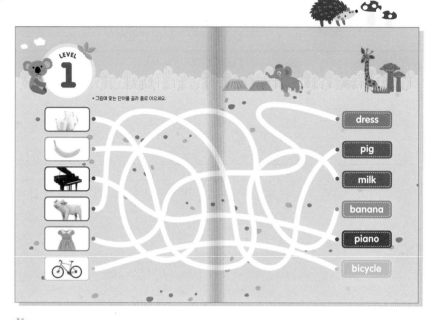

🌸 교육부 지정 초등필수 영단어 600 단어를 차근 차근 배워요!

초등학교 영어 교과서 권장 어휘 중 600개의 단어를 엄선해, 일상생활, 학교생활 등
주제별로 묶었습니다. 또 난이도에 따라 레벨을 분류해 놓아 성취감을 높일 수 있습니다.

하루 미션을
마치면 스티커를
붙여 성취감을
높이세요!

🌸 매일 매일 한 장씩 쉬운 공부습관을 만들어요!

하루에 한 장씩 10개의 단어를 60일 동안 꾸준히 학습하면,
두 달만에 초등필수 영단어를 마스터할 수 있습니다.

🌷 그림을 보고, 발음을 들으며 단어를 통으로 외워요!

주제별 단어가 그림과 함께 있어서 단어를 통으로 익힐 수 있습니다. 여기에 원어민이 녹음한 발음을 듣고 따라 하면 발음까지 한번에 익힐 수 있습니다.

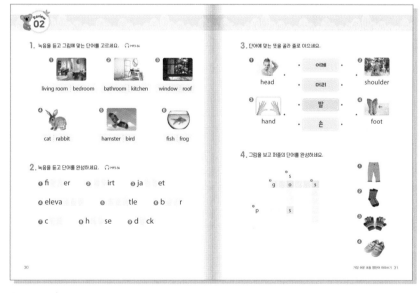

🌷 다양한 게임으로 재미있게 공부해요!

5일에 한 번씩 배운 단어를 복습하며 자신감을 높일 수 있습니다.
다양한 유형의 문제로 쉽고 재미있게 단어를 복습해 보세요.

▶ 그림에 맞는 단어를 골라 줄로 이으세요.

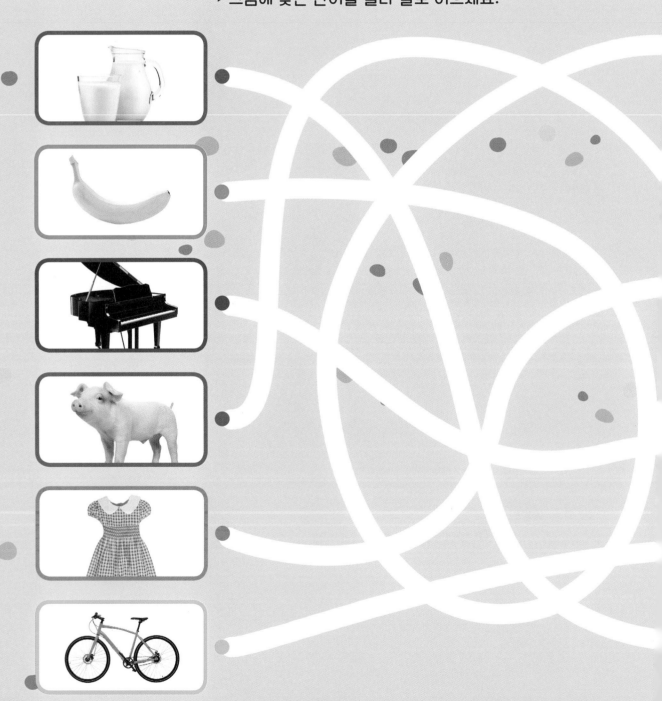

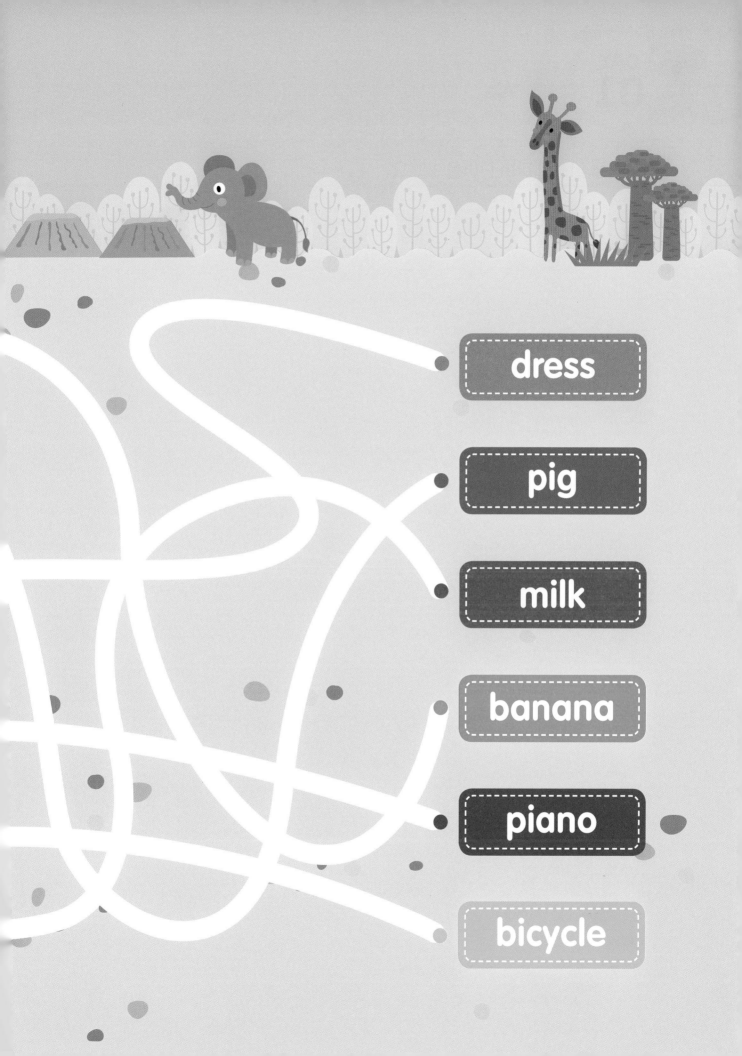

dress

pig

milk

banana

piano

bicycle

 월   일

오전   :
오후

🌷 녹음을 따라 말하며 단어를 쓰세요. 🎧 MP3-01

나

I I I I

너, 너희들

you you you you

우리

we we we we

그(남자)

he he he he

그녀(여자)

she she she she

그들

they they they they

10

그것

it it it it

이것

this this this this

저것

that that that that

모두

everyone everyone everyone

 그림에 맞는 단어를 완성하세요.

❶

❷

❸

e

e

th

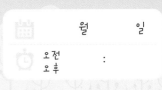 월   일

오 전
오 후   :

 녹음을 따라 말하며 단어를 쓰세요. 🎧 MP3-02

mother mother mother

 엄마

father father father

아빠

parents parents parents

부모님

brother brother brother

형(오빠), 남동생

sister sister sister sister

누나(언니),
여동생

grandparents grandparents

조부모님

grandfather grandfather

할아버지

grandmother grandmother

할머니

aunt aunt aunt aunt

고모(이모)

uncle uncle uncle uncle

삼촌

 그림에 맞는 단어를 완성하세요.

❶

par ☐☐ **ts**

❷

a ☐☐ **t**

❸

☐☐ **cle**

🌷 녹음을 따라 말하며 단어를 쓰세요. 🎧 MP3-03

안녕.

Hi. Hi. Hi. Hi.

잘 가.

Bye. Bye. Bye. Bye.

좋은 아침.

Good morning. Good morning.

좋은 오후.

Good afternoon. Good afternoon.

좋은 저녁.

Good evening. Good evening.

잘 자.

Good night. Good night.

You're welcome. You're welcome.

천만에요.

It's fine. It's fine. It's fine.

괜찮아요.

Okay. Okay. Okay. Okay.

좋아요.

Thank you. Thank you.

고마워요.

  그림에 맞는 단어를 완성하세요.

❶  **❷**  **❸**

B **.**   **Good morn** **.**   **Ok** **.**

월   일

오전
오후   :

 녹음을 따라 말하며 단어를 쓰세요. 🎧 MP3-04

1, 하나

one one one one

2, 둘

two two two two

3, 셋

three three three three

4, 넷

four four four four

5, 다섯

five five five five

6, 여섯

six six six six

7

7, 일곱

seven seven seven seven

8

8, 여덟

eight eight eight eight

9

9, 아홉

nine nine nine nine

10

10, 열

ten ten ten ten

 그림에 맞는 단어를 완성하세요.

❶

f ☐ ☐ r

❷

se ☐ ☐ n

❸

☐ ☐ ght

 녹음을 따라 말하며 단어를 쓰세요.　🎧 MP3-05

이마

forehead forehead forehead

눈

eye eye eye eye

코

nose nose nose nose

입

mouth mouth mouth mouth

귀

ear ear ear ear

입술

lip lip lip lip

tooth tooth tooth tooth

이빨, 치아

eyebrow eyebrow eyebrow

눈썹

cheek cheek cheek cheek

뺨

chin chin chin chin

턱

 그림에 맞는 단어를 완성하세요.

❶

too▢▢

❷

▢▢**eek**

❸

▢▢**in**

가장 쉬운 초등 영단어 따라쓰기 19

1. 녹음을 듣고 그림에 맞는 단어를 고르세요. 🎧 MP3-review 01-1

❶

mother | father

❷

brother | sister

❸

grandfather | grandmother

❹

two | three

❺

five | six

❻

nine | ten

2. 녹음을 듣고 단어를 완성하세요. 🎧 MP3-review 01-2

❶ H   .   ❷ li   ❸ eyebr

❹ y   ❺   is   ❻ th

❼ e   ryone   ❽ Good aftern   n.

❾ You're   come.

3. 단어에 맞는 뜻을 골라 줄로 이으세요.

① eye

귀

입

코

눈

② nose

③ mouth

④ ear

4. 그림을 보고 퍼즐의 단어를 완성하세요.

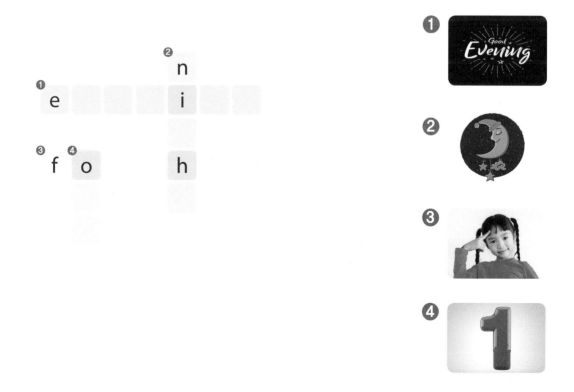

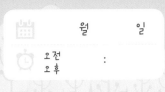

DAY 06 Body

🌷 녹음을 따라 말하며 단어를 쓰세요. 🎧 MP3-06

머리

head head head head

머리카락

hair hair hair hair

목

neck neck neck neck

어깨

shoulder shoulder shoulder

팔

arm arm arm arm

손

hand hand hand hand

finger finger finger finger

손가락

leg leg leg leg

다리

foot foot foot foot

발

toe toe toe toe

발가락

 그림에 맞는 단어를 완성하세요.

❶

h ▢ ▢ r

❷

ne ▢ ▢

❸

le ▢

 녹음을 따라 말하며 단어를 쓰세요. 🎧 MP3-07

shirt   shirt   shirt   shirt

셔츠(윗옷)

pants   pants   pants   pants

바지

blouse   blouse   blouse blouse

블라우스

skirt   skirt   skirt   skirt

치마

dress   dress   dress   dress

드레스, 원피스

jeans   jeans   jeans   jeans

청바지

jacket jacket jacket jacket

외투

socks socks socks socks

양말

gloves gloves gloves gloves

장갑

shoes shoes shoes shoes

신발

 그림에 맞는 단어를 완성하세요.

❶

sk　t

❷

dre

❸

j　ns

 녹음을 따라 말하며 단어를 쓰세요. 🎧 MP3-08

문

door door door door

방

room room room room

거실

living room living room

침실

bedroom bedroom bedroom

욕실

bathroom bathroom

부엌

kitchen kitchen kitchen

wall wall wall wall

벽

window window window

창문

roof roof roof roof

지붕

elevator elevator elevator

엘리베이터

 그림에 맞는 단어를 완성하세요.

❶

d ☐☐ **r**

❷

r ☐☐ **m**

❸

wa ☐☐

 녹음을 따라 말하며 단어를 쓰세요. 🎧 MP3-09

강아지

dog dog dog dog

고양이

cat cat cat cat

토끼

rabbit rabbit rabbit rabbit

햄스터

hamster hamster hamster

새

bird bird bird bird

물고기

fish fish fish fish

turtle turtle turtle turtle

거북이

frog frog frog frog

개구리

snake snake snake snake

뱀

iguana iguana iguana

이구아나

 그림에 맞는 단어를 완성하세요.

❶

do

❷

sn ke

❸

** gu na**

DAY 10

Animals (1)

 녹음을 따라 말하며 단어를 쓰세요. 🎧 MP3-10

tiger tiger tiger tiger

호랑이

lion lion lion lion

사자

bear bear bear bear

곰

wolf wolf wolf wolf

늑대

fox fox fox fox

여우

cow cow cow cow

소

30

horse horse horse horse

말

sheep sheep sheep sheep

양

duck duck duck duck

오리

pig pig pig pig

돼지

 그림에 맞는 단어를 완성하세요.

❶

ti ▮ **er**

❷

wol ▮

❸

pi ▮

1. 녹음을 듣고 그림에 맞는 단어를 고르세요. 🎧 MP3-review 02-1

❶
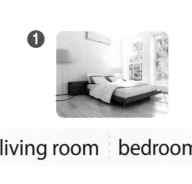
living room · bedroom

❷
bathroom · kitchen

❸

window · roof

❹

cat · rabbit

❺

hamster · bird

❻

fish · frog

2. 녹음을 듣고 단어를 완성하세요. 🎧 MP3-review 02-2

❶ fi____er ❷ ____irt ❸ ja____et

❹ eleva____ ❺ ____tle ❻ b____r

❼ c____ ❽ h____se ❾ d____ck

3. 단어에 맞는 뜻을 골라 줄로 이으세요.

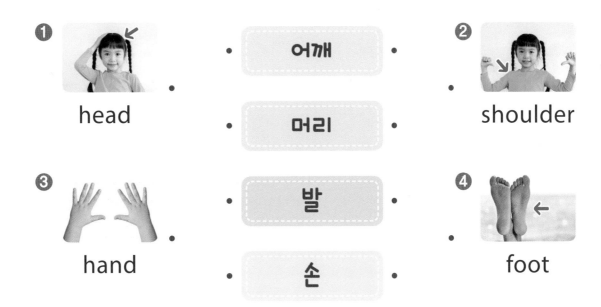

① head

어깨

머리

② shoulder

③ hand

발

손

④ foot

4. 그림을 보고 퍼즐의 단어를 완성하세요.

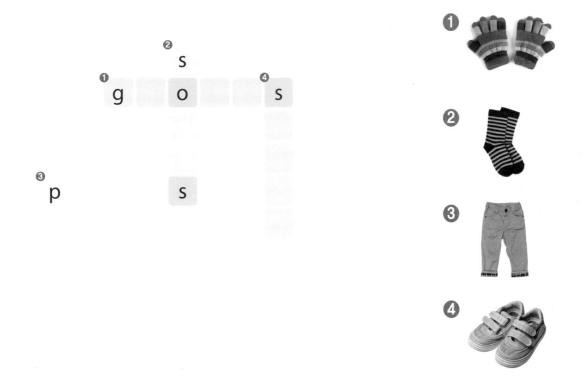

DAY 11 Food

 녹음을 따라 말하며 단어를 쓰세요. 🎧 MP3-11

밥, 쌀

rice rice rice rice

빵

bread bread bread bread

샌드위치

sandwich sandwich

치즈

cheese cheese cheese

잼

jam jam jam jam

버터

butter butter butter butter

34

tea tea tea tea

차

milk milk milk milk

우유

juice juice juice juice

주스

water water water water

물

 그림에 맞는 단어를 완성하세요.

①

br⬜⬜**d**

②

t⬜⬜

③

mil⬜

Fruits

 녹음을 따라 말하며 단어를 쓰세요.　🎧 MP3-12

사과

apple apple apple apple

배

pear pear pear pear

복숭아

peach peach peach peach

오렌지

orange orange orange

포도

grape grape grape grape

딸기

strawberry strawberry

36

banana banana banana

바나나

kiwi kiwi kiwi kiwi

키위

cherry cherry cherry cherry

체리

watermelon watermelon

수박

 그림에 맞는 단어를 완성하세요.

❶

a ☐ ☐ le

❷

k ☐ w ☐

❸

che ☐ ☐ ☐

월   일

오전 :
오후

 녹음을 따라 말하며 단어를 쓰세요. MP3-13

배추

cabbage cabbage cabbage

옥수수

corn corn corn corn

감자

potato potato potato

고구마

sweet potato sweet potato

양파

onion onion onion onion

당근

carrot carrot carrot carrot

pumpkin pumpkin pumpkin

호박

cucumber cucumber

오이

bean bean bean bean

콩

chili chili chili chili

고추

 그림에 맞는 단어를 완성하세요.

❶

❷

❸

ca▢▢age　　　**sw▢▢t p▢tat▢**　　　**ch▢l**

월   일
오전   :
오후

 녹음을 따라 말하며 단어를 쓰세요.   MP3-14

rose rose rose rose

장미

tulip tulip tulip tulip

튤립

lily lily lily lily

백합

sunflower sunflower

해바라기

cosmos cosmos cosmos

코스모스

morning glory morning glory

나팔꽃

carnation carnation

카네이션

leaf leaf leaf leaf

잎

seed seed seed seed

씨, 씨앗

root root root root

뿌리

 그림에 맞는 단어를 완성하세요.

❶

⬜⬜ se

❷

lil⬜

❸

c ⬜ m ⬜ s

DAY 15   Colors

 녹음을 따라 말하며 단어를 쓰세요.   🎧 MP3-15

red   red   red   red

빨간색

blue   blue   blue   blue

파란색

yellow   yellow   yellow   yellow

노란색

green   green   green   green

초록색

purple   purple   purple   purple

보라색

pink   pink   pink   pink

분홍색

brown brown brown brown

갈색

gray gray gray gray

회색

black black black black

검은색

white white white white

흰색

 그림에 맞는 단어를 완성하세요.

❶

pu **pl**

❷

bla

❸

ite

1. 녹음을 듣고 그림에 맞는 단어를 고르세요. 🎧 MP3-review 03-1

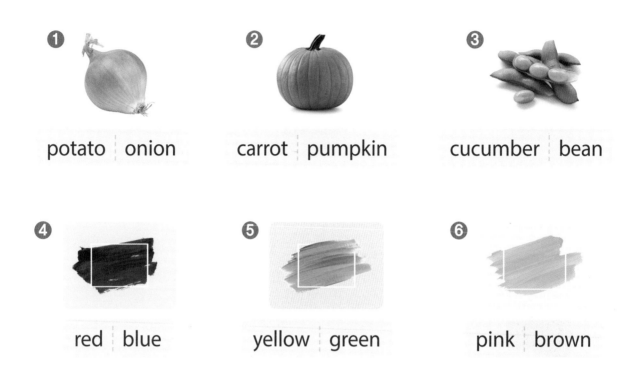

❶ potato ┊ onion

❷ carrot ┊ pumpkin

❸ cucumber ┊ bean

❹ red ┊ blue

❺ yellow ┊ green

❻ pink ┊ brown

2. 녹음을 듣고 단어를 완성하세요. 🎧 MP3-review 03-2

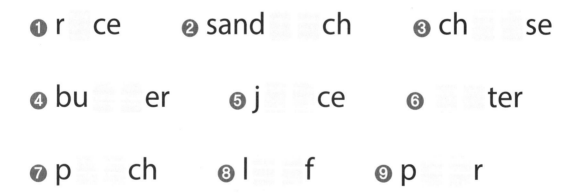

❶ r　ce　　❷ sand　ch　　❸ ch　　se

❹ bu　　er　　❺ j　ce　　❻ 　ter

❼ p　ch　　❽ l　f　　❾ p　r

3. 단어에 맞는 뜻을 골라 줄로 이으세요.

❶ orange

바나나

딸기

포도

오렌지

❷ grape

❸ strawberry

❹ banana

4. 그림을 보고 퍼즐의 단어를 완성하세요.

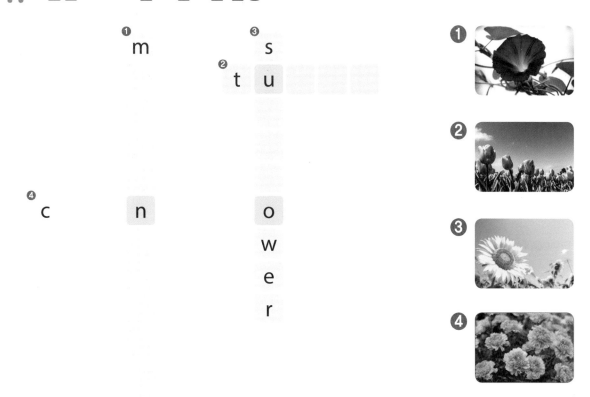

❶ m

❸ s

❷ t u

❹ c　n

o
w
e
r

❶
❷
❸
❹

 녹음을 따라 말하며 단어를 쓰세요. 🎧 MP3-16

피아노

piano piano piano piano

기타

guitar guitar guitar guitar

드럼

drum drum drum drum

탬버린

tambourine tambourine

트라이앵글

triangle triangle triangle

캐스터네츠

castanets castanets

violin violin violin violin

바이올린

cello cello cello cello

첼로

trumpet trumpet trumpet

트럼펫

flute flute flute flute

플루트

 그림에 맞는 단어를 완성하세요.

❶

g▢▢**tar**

❷

viol▢▢

❸

flu▢▢

오전
오후

🌷 녹음을 따라 말하며 단어를 쓰세요. 🎧 MP3-17

공

ball ball ball ball

인형

doll doll doll doll

장난감

toy toy toy toy

상자

box box box box

컴퓨터

computer computer

방망이

bat bat bat bat

book book book book

책

umbrella umbrella umbrella

우산

glasses glasses glasses

안경

ring ring ring ring

고리

 그림에 맞는 단어를 완성하세요.

❶
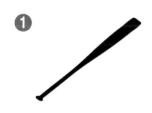

b ☐ **t**

❷

b ☐ ☐ **k**

❸

gla ☐ ☐ **es**

월   일
오전
오후   :

 녹음을 따라 말하며 단어를 쓰세요. 🎧 MP3-18

자동차

car car car car

버스

bus bus bus bus

지하철

subway subway subway

기차

train train train train

자전거

bicycle bicycle bicycle

오토바이

motorcycle motorcycle

truck truck truck truck

트럭

ship ship ship ship

배

airplane airplane airplane

비행기

helicopter helicopter

헬리콥터

 그림에 맞는 단어를 완성하세요.

❶

c▢▢

❷

subw▢▢

❸

bi▢▢**cle**

 녹음을 따라 말하며 단어를 쓰세요. 🎧 MP3-19

행복한

happy happy happy

슬픈

sad sad sad sad

사랑하다

love love love love

싫어하다

hate hate hate hate

놀란

surprised surprised surprised

피곤한

tired tired tired tired

angry angry angry angry

화난

glad glad glad glad

기쁜

bored bored bored bored

지루한

excited excited excited

신나는

 그림에 맞는 단어를 완성하세요.

❶

sa☐

❷

lo☐e

❸

ha☐e

가장 쉬운 초등 영단어 따라쓰기 53

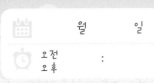
 녹음을 따라 말하며 단어를 쓰세요. 🎧 MP3-20

go go go go

가다

stop stop stop stop

멈추다

stand stand stand stand

서다

sit sit sit sit

앉다

open open open open

열다

close close close close

닫다

come come come come

오다

meet meet meet meet

만나다

like like like like

좋아하다

have have have have

갖다

 그림에 맞는 단어를 완성하세요.

①

②

③

s ☐ t   op ☐ n   clo ☐ ☐

1. 녹음을 듣고 그림에 맞는 단어를 고르세요. 🎧 MP3-review 04-1

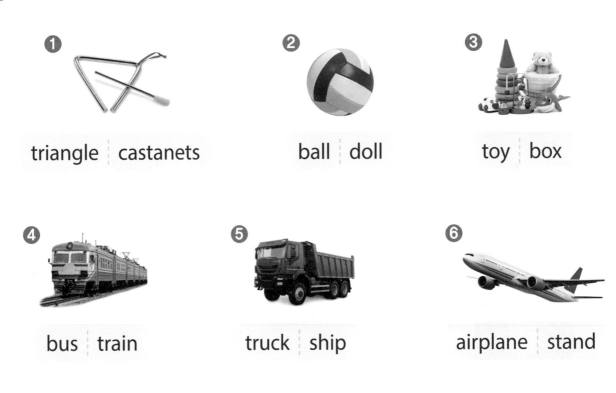

❶ triangle ┆ castanets

❷ ball ┆ doll

❸ toy ┆ box

❹ bus ┆ train

❺ truck ┆ ship

❻ airplane ┆ stand

2. 녹음을 듣고 단어를 완성하세요. 🎧 MP3-review 04-2

❶ ha   ❷ s   prised   ❸ t   ed

❹ ang   ❺ b   ed   ❻   cited

❼ c   me   ❽ m   t   ❾ l   ke

3. 단어에 맞는 뜻을 골라 줄로 이으세요.

❶ piano

트럼펫

탬버린

드럼

피아노

❷ drum

❸ tambourine

❹ trumpet

4. 그림을 보고 퍼즐의 단어를 완성하세요.

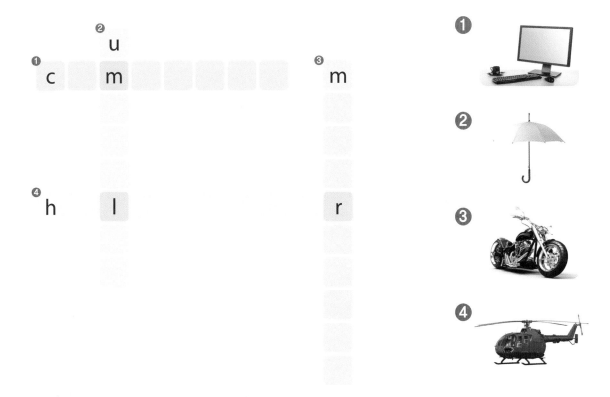

▸ 그림에 맞는 단어를 골라 줄로 이으세요.

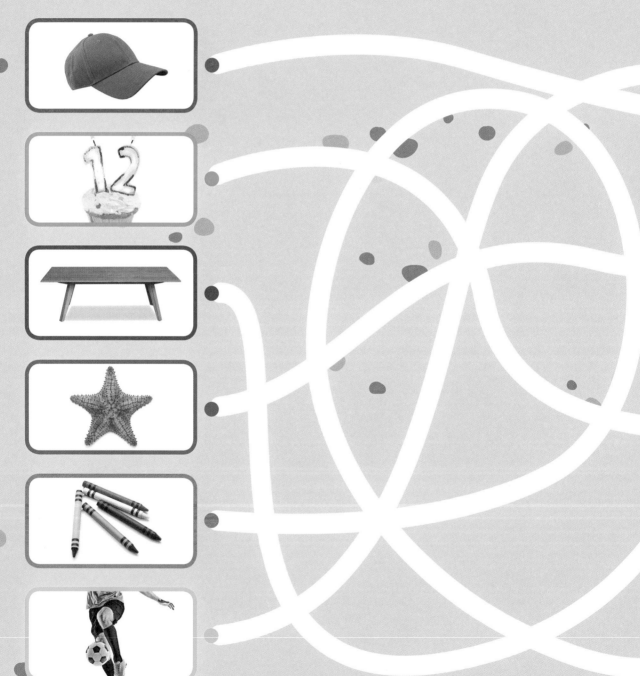

cap

starfish

crayon

soccer

table

twelve

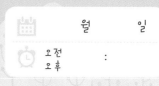

 녹음을 따라 말하며 단어를 쓰세요. 🎧 MP3-21

baby baby baby baby

아기

child child child child

어린이

boy boy boy boy

남자 아이

girl girl girl girl

여자 아이

man man man man

남자(어른)

woman woman woman

여자(어른)

신사

gentleman gentleman

숙녀

lady lady lady lady

사람

person person person

사람들

people people people

 그림에 맞는 단어를 완성하세요.

①

bab ▢

②

l ▢ **dy**

③

p ▢ ▢ **ple**

 녹음을 따라 말하며 단어를 쓰세요.   🎧 MP3-22

coat   coat   coat   coat

코트

button   button   button

단추

pocket   pocket   pocket

주머니

vest   vest   vest   vest

조끼

sweater   sweater   sweater

스웨터

shorts   shorts   shorts   shorts

반바지

belt belt belt belt

허리띠

cap cap cap cap

모자

boots boots boots boots

부츠

handkerchief handkerchief

손수건

 그림에 맞는 단어를 완성하세요.

❶

sh **ts**

❷

b **lt**

❸

ca

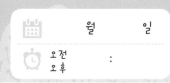

 녹음을 따라 말하며 단어를 쓰세요. 🎧 MP3-23

eleven eleven eleven eleven

11, 열하나

twelve twelve twelve twelve

12, 열둘

thirteen thirteen thirteen

13, 열셋

fourteen fourteen fourteen

14, 열넷

fifteen fifteen fifteen fifteen

15, 열다섯

sixteen sixteen sixteen

16, 열여섯

seventeen seventeen

17, 열일곱

eighteen eighteen eighteen

18, 열여덟

nineteen nineteen nineteen

19, 열아홉

twenty twenty twenty twenty

20, 스물

 그림에 맞는 단어를 완성하세요.

❶

eight ⬜⬜**n**

❷

ninet ⬜⬜**n**

❸

t ⬜ ⬜ **nty**

월   일
오전   :
오후

 녹음을 따라 말하며 단어를 쓰세요. 🎧 MP3-24

커튼

curtain curtain curtain

소파

sofa sofa sofa sofa

탁자

table table table table

텔레비전

television television

전화기

telephone telephone

침대

bed bed bed bed

베개

pillow pillow pillow pillow

이불

blanket blanket blanket

벽장

closet closet closet closet

서랍장

drawer drawer drawer

 그림에 맞는 단어를 완성하세요.

❶

so **a**

❷

ta **le**

❸

be

 녹음을 따라 말하며 단어를 쓰세요. 🎧 MP3-25

욕조

bathtub bathtub bathtub

변기

toilet toilet toilet toilet

샤워

shower shower shower

비누

soap soap soap soap

샴푸

shampoo shampoo

냉장고

refrigerator refrigerator

stove stove stove stove

레인지

spoon spoon spoon spoon

숟가락

chopsticks chopsticks

젓가락

cup cup cup cup

컵

 그림에 맞는 단어를 완성하세요.

❶

sh◻◻**er**

❷

s◻◻**p**

❸

sto◻◻

1. 녹음을 듣고 그림에 맞는 단어를 고르세요. 🎧 MP3-review 05-1

① boy | girl

② man | woman

③ television | telephone

④ eleven | twelve

⑤ thirteen | fifteen

⑥ pillow | blanket

2. 녹음을 듣고 단어를 완성하세요. 🎧 MP3-review 05-2

① butt ⬜⬜

② po ⬜ et

③ s ⬜ ter

④ b ⬜ ts

⑤ batht ⬜⬜

⑥ t ⬜ let

⑦ sham ⬜⬜

⑧ ch ⬜ sticks

⑨ cl ⬜ set

3. 단어에 맞는 뜻을 골라 줄로 이으세요.

❶ child

숟가락

코트

❷ coat

❸ spoon

컵

아이

❹ cup

4. 그림을 보고 퍼즐의 단어를 완성하세요.

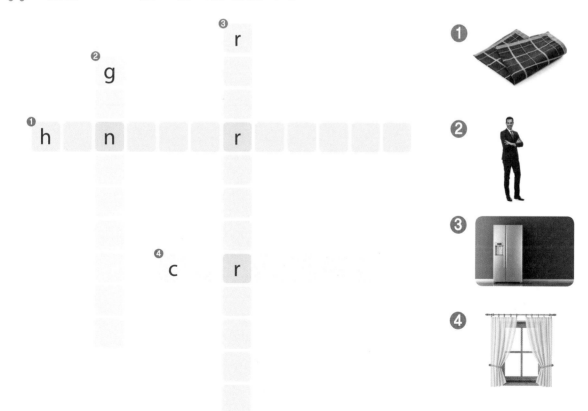

❸ r

❷ g

❶ h · n · · · r · · · ·

❹ c · r

❶

❷

❸

❹

 녹음을 따라 말하며 단어를 쓰세요. 🎧 MP3-26

아침 식사

breakfast breakfast

점심 식사

lunch lunch lunch lunch

저녁 식사

dinner dinner dinner dinner

달걀

egg egg egg egg

샐러드

salad salad salad salad

맛있는

delicious delicious delicious

sweet sweet sweet sweet

달콤한

bitter bitter bitter bitter

쓴

eat eat eat eat

먹다

drink drink drink drink

마시다

 그림에 맞는 단어를 완성하세요.

❶

delici◻◻◻

❷

sw◻◻**t**

❸

bitt◻**r**

 녹음을 따라 말하며 단어를 쓰세요. 🎧 MP3-27

elephant　elephant　elephant

코끼리

giraffe　giraffe　giraffe

기린

kangaroo　kangaroo

캥거루

gorilla　gorilla　gorilla　gorilla

고릴라

panda　panda　panda　panda

판다

deer　deer　deer　deer

사슴

camel camel camel camel

낙타

monkey monkey monkey

원숭이

ostrich ostrich ostrich

타조

zebra zebra zebra zebra

얼룩말

 그림에 맞는 단어를 완성하세요.

❶

gori▢▢▢

❷

p▢▢**da**

❸

d▢▢**r**

오전 :
오후

 녹음을 따라 말하며 단어를 쓰세요. 🎧 MP3-28

고래

whale whale whale whale

상어

shark shark shark shark

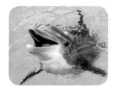
돌고래

dolphin dolphin dolphin

물개

seal seal seal seal

펭귄

penguin penguin penguin

오징어

squid squid squid squid

octopus octopus octopus

문어

crab crab crab crab

게, 가재

shrimp shrimp shrimp

새우

starfish starfish starfish

불가사리

 그림에 맞는 단어를 완성하세요.

❶

❷

❸

☐☐ale   octop☐☐   sh☐☐mp

 녹음을 따라 말하며 단어를 쓰세요. 🎧 MP3-29

color color color color

색, 색칠하다

brush brush brush brush

붓

crayon crayon crayon

크레파스

paint paint paint paint

물감

make make make make

만들다

cut cut cut cut

자르다

line line line line

선

circle circle circle circle

동그라미

triangle triangle triangle

세모

square square square

네모

🌷 그림에 맞는 단어를 완성하세요.

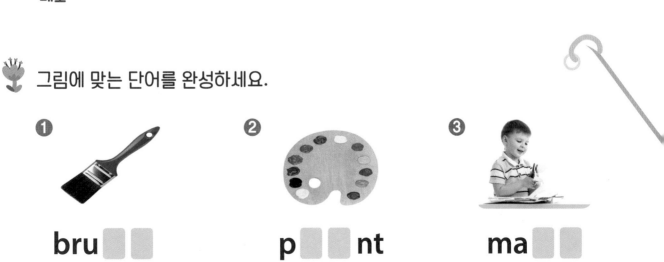

❶ **bru**⬜⬜

❷ **p**⬜⬜**nt**

❸ **ma**⬜⬜

월   일
오전
오후   :

 녹음을 따라 말하며 단어를 쓰세요. 🎧 MP3-30

can can can can

통

vase vase vase vase

꽃병

album album album album

앨범

clock clock clock clock

시계

picture picture picture

그림

photo photo photo photo

사진

fan fan fan fan

선풍기

lamp lamp lamp lamp

등, 등불

flag flag flag flag

깃발

key key key key

열쇠

 그림에 맞는 단어를 완성하세요.

❶
pic　　re

❷
**　　oto**

❸
f　n

1. 녹음을 듣고 그림에 맞는 단어를 고르세요. 🎧 MP3-review 06-1

① egg · salad

② elephant · giraffe

③ crab · starfish

④ line · circle

⑤ triangle · square

⑥ clock · lamp

2. 녹음을 듣고 단어를 완성하세요. 🎧 MP3-review 06-2

① ☐ t   **②** d ☐ nk   **③** monk ☐

④ sh ☐ k   **⑤** sq ☐ d   **⑥** ☐ se

⑦ al ☐ um   **⑧** c t   **⑨** k ☐

3. 단어에 맞는 뜻을 골라 줄로 이으세요.

❶ zebra

• 깃발 •

• 돌고래 •

❷ dolphin

❸ crayon

• 크레파스 •

• 얼룩말 •

❹ flag

4. 그림을 보고 퍼즐의 단어를 완성하세요.

❶ b ☐ ☐ ☐ ❷ k ☐ ☐ ☐ ☐

❸ p ☐ n

❹ o ☐ ☐ ☐ r

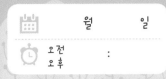
 녹음을 따라 말하며 단어를 쓰세요.　🎧 MP3-31

초

second　second　second

분

minute　minute　minute

시

hour　hour　hour　hour

날, 일

day　day　day　day

주

week　week　week　week

주말

weekend　weekend　weekend

month month month month

달

year year year year

해, 년

calendar calendar calendar

달력

date date date date

날짜

 그림에 맞는 단어를 완성하세요.

❶

mon

❷

ar

❸

d te

 녹음을 따라 말하며 단어를 쓰세요. 🎧 MP3-32

January January January

1월

February February February

2월

March March March March

3월

April April April April

4월

May May May May

5월

June June June June

6월

July July July July

7월

August August August

8월

September September

9월

October October October

10월

 그림에 맞는 단어를 완성하세요.

❶

Aug st

❷

S **tember**

❸

tober

 녹음을 따라 말하며 단어를 쓰세요.　🎧 MP3-33

11월

November November

12월

December December

봄

spring spring spring spring

여름

summer summer summer

가을

fall fall fall fall

겨울

winter winter winter winter

휴일

holiday · holiday · holiday

방학, 휴가

vacation · vacation · vacation

추수감사절

Thanksgiving Day · Thanksgiving Day

크리스마스

Christmas · Christmas

 그림에 맞는 단어를 완성하세요.

1

hol□day

2

□□cation

3

Chri□□mas

오 전
오 후

 녹음을 따라 말하며 단어를 쓰세요.   🎧 MP3-34

sky   sky   sky   sky

하늘

land   land   land   land

땅

sea   sea   sea   sea

바다

river   river   river   river

강

sun   sun   sun   sun

해

moon   moon   moon   moon

달

star star star star

별

storm storm storm storm

폭풍

thunder thunder thunder

번개

rainbow rainbow rainbow

무지개

  그림에 맞는 단어를 완성하세요.

❶

❷

❸

sk■   **lan**■   ■■**under**

 녹음을 따라 말하며 단어를 쓰세요. 🎧 MP3-35

축구

soccer   soccer   soccer

야구

baseball   baseball   baseball

농구

basketball   basketball

배구

volleyball   volleyball

테니스

tennis   tennis   tennis   tennis

탁구

table tennis   table tennis

배드민턴

badminton badminton

볼링

bowling bowling bowling

스키

ski ski ski ski

스케이트

skate skate skate skate

 그림에 맞는 단어를 완성하세요.

1

2

3

so ⬜⬜ **er**   **ba** ⬜⬜ **ball**   **s** ⬜⬜ **te**

1. 녹음을 듣고 그림에 맞는 단어를 고르세요. 🎧 MP3-review 07-1

❶ day | week

❷ November | December

❸ moon | star

❹ January | February

❺ April | May

❻ June | July

2. 녹음을 듣고 단어를 완성하세요. 🎧 MP3-review 07-2

❶ sec　d　　❷ mi　te　　❸ h　r

❹ s　　　❺ ri　r　　❻ s　n

❼ rainb　　　❽ 　lleyball　　❾ te　is

3. 단어에 맞는 뜻을 골라 줄로 이으세요.

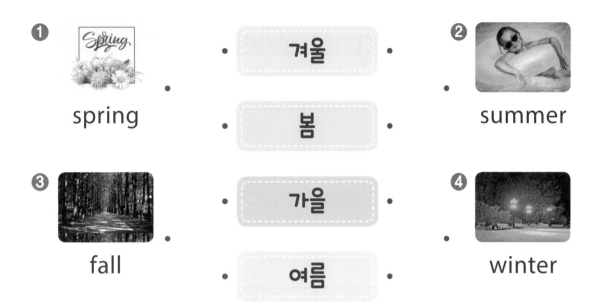

① spring

겨울

봄

② summer

③ fall

가을

여름

④ winter

4. 그림을 보고 퍼즐의 단어를 완성하세요.

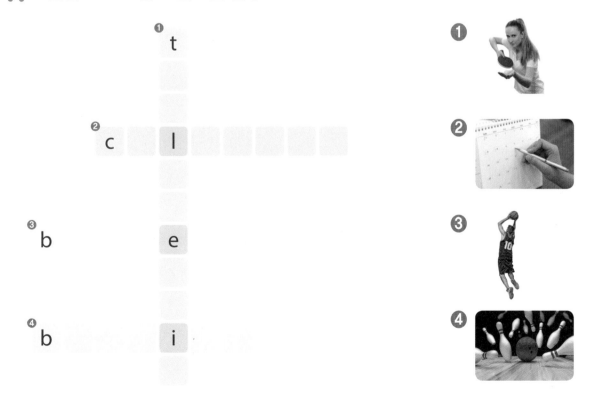

① t

② c   l

③ b   e

④ b   i

DAY 36

Hobbies

 녹음을 따라 말하며 단어를 쓰세요. 🎧 MP3-36

요리

cooking cooking cooking

춤추다

dance dance dance dance

노래하다

sing sing sing sing

그리다

draw draw draw draw

영화

movie movie movie movie

camera

카메라

camera camera camera

kite kite kite kite

연

jogging jogging jogging

달리기, 조깅

travel travel travel travel

여행하다

play play play play

놀다

 그림에 맞는 단어를 완성하세요.

❶

c ☐ ☐ king

❷

dr ☐ ☐

❸

tra ☐ ☐ l

 녹음을 따라 말하며 단어를 쓰세요. 🎧 MP3-37

cook cook cook cook

요리사

doctor doctor doctor doctor

의사

nurse nurse nurse nurse

간호사

scientist scientist scientist

과학자

farmer farmer farmer

농부

police officer police officer

경찰관

98

writer writer writer writer

작가

artist artist artist artist

화가, 예술가

musician musician musician

음악가

model model model model

모델

 그림에 맞는 단어를 완성하세요.

❶

n ☐ ☐ se

❷

sc ☐ ☐ ntist

❸

musi ☐ ☐ an

DAY 38 Looks

 녹음을 따라 말하며 단어를 쓰세요. 🎧 MP3-38

새로운

new new new new

오래된

old old old old

키가 큰

tall tall tall tall

예쁜

pretty pretty pretty pretty

아름다운

beautiful beautiful beautiful

못생긴

ugly ugly ugly ugly

무거운

heavy heavy heavy heavy

가벼운

light light light light

밝은

bright bright bright bright

어두운

dark dark dark dark

 그림에 맞는 단어를 완성하세요.

❶

n ▢▢

❷

ta ▢▢

❸

pr ▢ **tty**

DAY 39 Feelings (2)

 녹음을 따라 말하며 단어를 쓰세요. 🎧 MP3-39

대단한

great great great great

나쁜

bad bad bad bad

기쁜

joyful joyful joyful joyful

걱정스러운

worried worried worried

무서운

scared scared scared

배고픈

hungry hungry hungry

full full full full

배부른

upset upset upset upset

속상한

thirsty thirsty thirsty thirsty

목마른

sleepy sleepy sleepy sleepy

졸린

 그림에 맞는 단어를 완성하세요.

❶

gr ⬜⬜ **t**

❷

⬜ **pset**

❸

slee ⬜⬜

DAY 40

Actions (2)

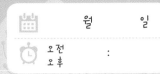

오전 오후

 녹음을 따라 말하며 단어를 쓰세요. 🎧 MP3-40

start start start start

시작하다

finish finish finish finish

마치다

move move move move

움직이다,
이동하다

continue continue continue

계속하다

call call call call

전화하다

walk walk walk walk

걷다

ride ride ride ride

(탈것을) **타다**

put put put put

넣다

fall fall fall fall

떨어지다

help help help help

돕다

 그림에 맞는 단어를 완성하세요.

❶

st▢▢t

❷

w▢▢k

❸

r▢de

1. 녹음을 듣고 그림에 맞는 단어를 고르세요. 🎧 MP3-review 08-1

❶

dance sing

❷

kite jogging

❸

writer artist

❹

heavy light

❺

joyful scared

❻

hungry full

2. 녹음을 듣고 단어를 완성하세요. 🎧 MP3-review 08-2

❶ mov ☐ ☐

❷ ☐ ly

❸ d ☐ k

❹ fa ☐ ☐

❺ he ☐ ☐

❻ fini ☐ ☐

❼ mo ☐ ☐

❽ contin ☐ ☐

❾ ca ☐ ☐

3. 단어에 맞는 뜻을 골라 줄로 이으세요.

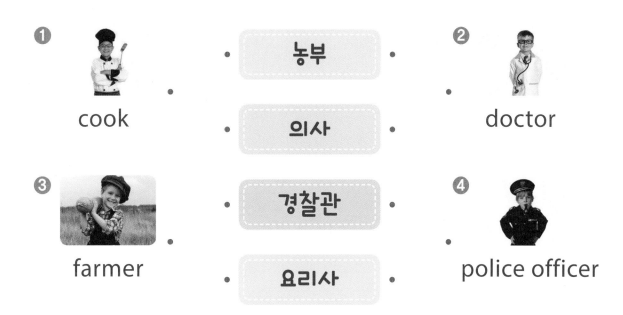

① cook

농부

의사

② doctor

③ farmer

경찰관

요리사

④ police officer

4. 그림을 보고 퍼즐의 단어를 완성하세요.

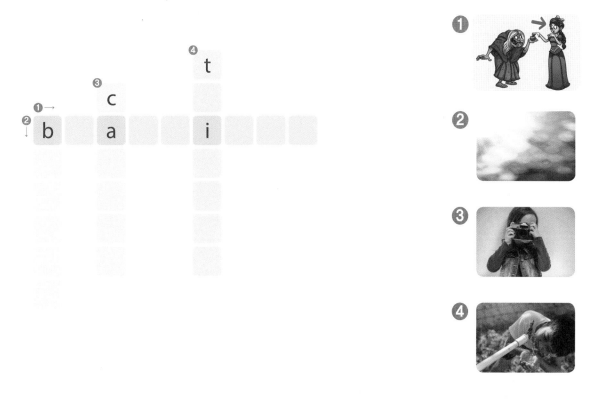

④ t

③ c

① →
② ↓ b a i

LEVEL

3

▶ 그림에 맞는 단어를 골라 줄로 이으세요.

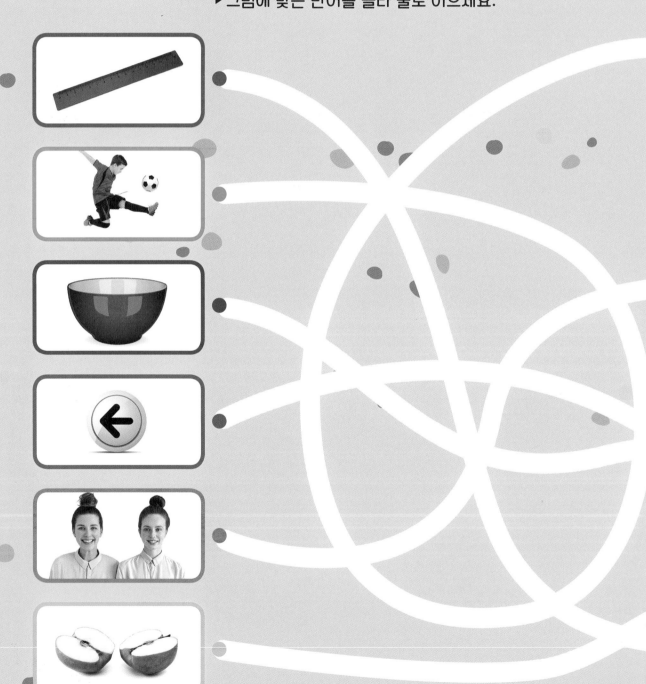

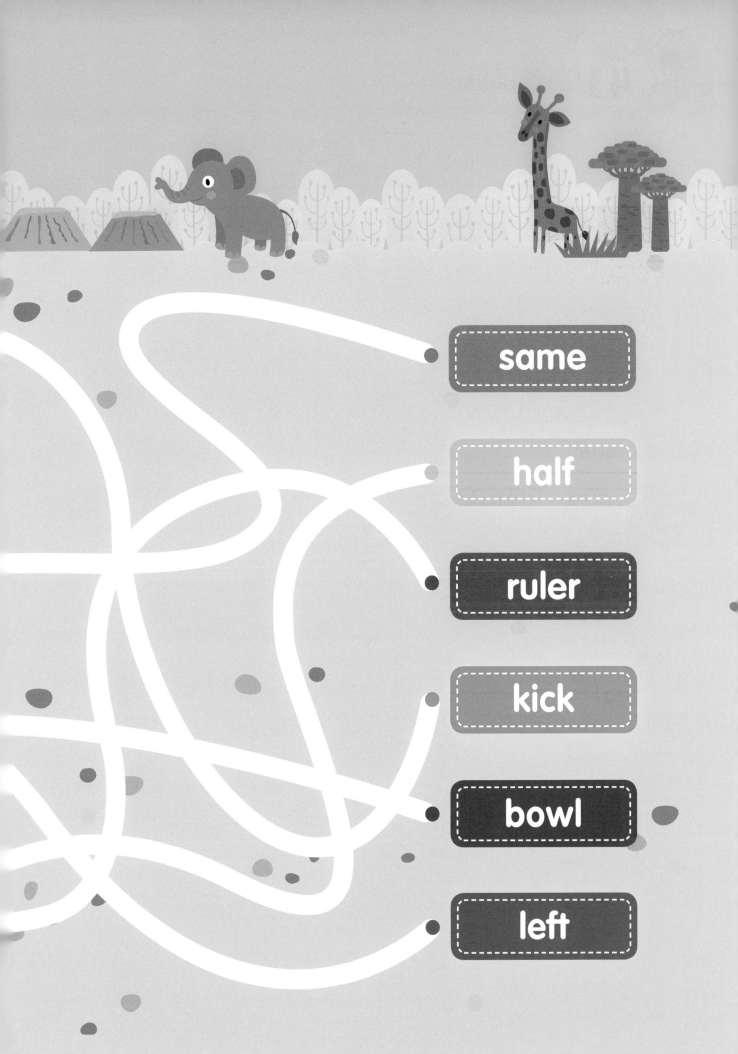

월   일
오전
오후   :

 녹음을 따라 말하며 단어를 쓰세요. 🎧 MP3-41

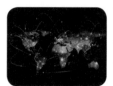

세계

world world world world

한국

Korea Korea Korea Korea

일본

Japan Japan Japan Japan

중국

China China China

인도

India India India India

미국

America America America

캐나다

Canada Canada Canada

독일

Germany Germany Germany

영국

England England England

프랑스

France France France

 그림에 맞는 단어를 완성하세요.

❶

❷

❸

　orea

　　ina

　merica

🌷 녹음을 따라 말하며 단어를 쓰세요. 🎧 MP3-42

store store store store

가게

restaurant restaurant

음식점

bakery bakery bakery

빵집

church church church

교회

library library library library

도서관

hospital hospital hospital

병원

약국

drugstore drugstore

극장

theater theater theater

은행

bank bank bank bank

우체국

post office post office

 그림에 맞는 단어를 완성하세요.

❶

bak☐☐y

❷

libr☐☐y

❸

☐☐eater

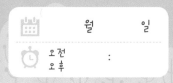
 녹음을 따라 말하며 단어를 쓰세요. 🎧 MP3-43

반

class class class class

선생님

teacher teacher teacher

학생

student student student

책상

desk desk desk desk

의자

chair chair chair chair

가방

bag bag bag bag

textbook textbook textbook

교과서

pencil pencil pencil pencil

연필

ruler ruler ruler ruler

자

note note note note

공책

 그림에 맞는 단어를 완성하세요.

❶ de☐☐

❷ ch☐☐r

❸ b☐g

DAY 44 **Playgrounds**

 녹음을 따라 말하며 단어를 쓰세요. 🎧 MP3-44

slide slide slide slide

미끄럼틀

swing swing swing swing

그네

jump jump jump jump

뛰다

throw throw throw throw

던지다

hide hide hide hide

숨다

find find find find

찾다

catch catch catch catch

잡다

shout shout shout shout

소리치다

hit hit hit hit

때리다, 치다

kick kick kick kick

차다

 그림에 맞는 단어를 완성하세요.

❶

sli ▢▢

❷

hi ▢▢

❸

fin ▢

월   일

오 전
오 후   :

 녹음을 따라 말하며 단어를 쓰세요. 🎧 MP3-45

소풍

picnic picnic picnic picnic

들판

field field field field

벤치

bench bench bench bench

연못

fountain fountain fountain

풍선

balloon balloon balloon

어린이

kid kid kid kid

trash can trash can

휴지통

run run run run

달리다

smile smile smile smile

웃다

relax relax relax relax

쉬다

  그림에 맞는 단어를 완성하세요.

❶

pi　nic

❷

r　n

❸

smi

1. 녹음을 듣고 그림에 맞는 단어를 고르세요. 🎧 MP3-review 09-1

① church ┊ hospital

② bank ┊ post office

③ bench ┊ fountain

④ jump ┊ throw

⑤ hit ┊ kick

⑥ pencil ┊ paper

2. 녹음을 듣고 단어를 완성하세요. 🎧 MP3-review 09-2

① w ▢ ld

② ▢ apan

③ ▢ anada

④ ▢ gland

⑤ Fran ▢

⑥ te ▢ book

⑦ cat ▢

⑧ f ▢ ld

⑨ rel ▢

3. 단어에 맞는 뜻을 골라 줄로 이으세요.

❶ store

풍선

자

❷ ruler

❸ swing

그네

가게

❹ balloon

4. 그림을 보고 퍼즐의 단어를 완성하세요.

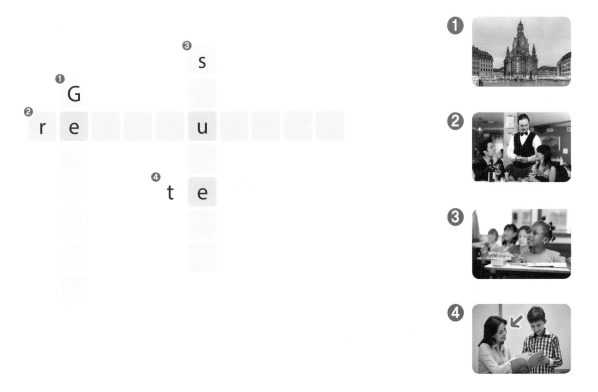

 녹음을 따라 말하며 단어를 쓰세요. 🎧 MP3-46

고기

meat meat meat meat

수프

soup soup soup soup

쇠고기

beef beef beef beef

닭고기

chicken chicken chicken

돼지고기

pork pork pork pork

사발

bowl bowl bowl bowl

dish dish dish dish

접시

sugar sugar sugar sugar

설탕

salt salt salt salt

소금

pepper pepper pepper

후추

 그림에 맞는 단어를 완성하세요.

❶
sou

❷
bee

❸
owl

DAY
47

Markets

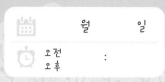

얼   일

오전
오후   :

 녹음을 따라 말하며 단어를 쓰세요. 🎧 MP3-47

식품

groceries groceries groceries

과자

snack snack snack snack

음료

beverage beverage beverage

사다

buy buy buy buy

팔다

sell sell sell sell

고르다

choose choose choose

가격

price price price price

무료

free free free free

싼

cheap cheap cheap cheap

비싼

expensive expensive

 그림에 맞는 단어를 완성하세요.

❶

gro [ ] [ ] **ries**

❷

[ ] [ ] **ack**

❸

be [ ] [ ] **rage**

 녹음을 따라 말하며 단어를 쓰세요. 🎧 MP3-48

숲

forest forest forest forest

정글

jungle jungle jungle jungle

언덕

hill hill hill hill

호수

lake lake lake lake

바위

rock rock rock rock

연못

pond pond pond pond

tree tree tree tree

나무

flower flower flower flower

꽃

climb climb climb climb

오르다

fresh fresh fresh fresh

상쾌한

 그림에 맞는 단어를 완성하세요.

❶

fo ▢ ▢ st

❷

▢ ▢ ke

❸

▢ ▢ ck

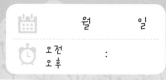
 녹음을 따라 말하며 단어를 쓰세요. 🎧 MP3-49

ocean ocean ocean ocean

바다

wave wave wave wave

파도

sand sand sand sand

모래

swim swim swim swim

수영하다

hat hat hat hat

모자

sunglasses sunglasses

선글라스

sunscreen sunscreen

자외선차단제

bottle bottle bottle bottle

물병

break break break break

쉬다

lie lie lie lie

눕다

 그림에 맞는 단어를 완성하세요.

❶

h ☐ t

❷

sungla ☐ ☐ es

❸

bo ☐ ☐ le

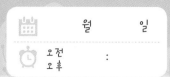
월   일
오전 :
오후

 녹음을 따라 말하며 단어를 쓰세요. 🎧 MP3-50

여기

here here here here

저기

there there there there

꼭대기

top top top top

중간

middle middle middle

바닥

bottom bottom bottom

구석, 모서리

corner corner corner

끝

end end end end

~ 앞쪽에

in front of in front of

~ 뒤에

behind behind behind

~ 옆에

next to next to next to

 그림에 맞는 단어를 완성하세요.

①

midd ☐ ☐

②

corn ☐ ☐

③

☐ nd

1. 녹음을 듣고 그림에 맞는 단어를 고르세요. 🎧 MP3-review 10-1

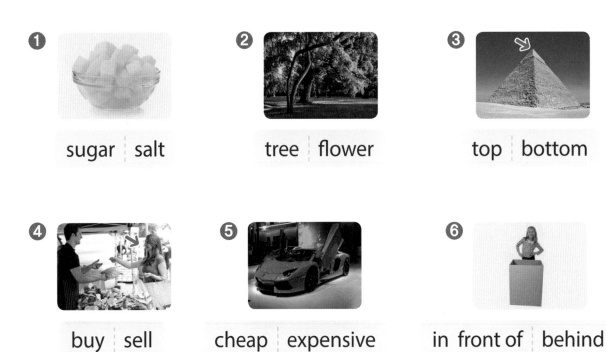

❶ sugar ┊ salt

❷ tree ┊ flower

❸ top ┊ bottom

❹ buy ┊ sell

❺ cheap ┊ expensive

❻ in front of ┊ behind

2. 녹음을 듣고 단어를 완성하세요. 🎧 MP3-review 10-2

❶ hi

❷ p   nd

❸ o   an

❹ wa

❺ san

❻ swi

❼ he

❽   ere

❾ br   k

3. 단어에 맞는 뜻을 골라 줄로 이으세요.

❶ pork

돼지고기

접시

정글

가격

❷ dish

❸ price

❹ jungle

4. 그림을 보고 퍼즐의 단어를 완성하세요.

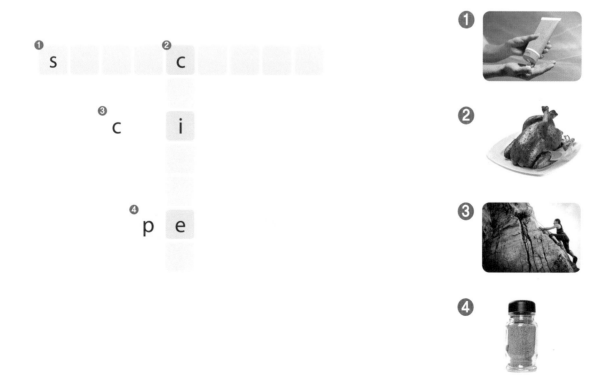

월   일

오전
오후   :

 녹음을 따라 말하며 단어를 쓰세요. 🎧 MP3-51

left left left left

왼쪽

right right right right

오른쪽

up up up up

위

down down down down

아래

east east east east

동쪽

west west west west

서쪽

남쪽

south south south south

북쪽

north north north north

곧장

straight straight straight

떨어져

away away away away

 그림에 맞는 단어를 완성하세요.

①

st

②

st

③

str ght

 녹음을 따라 말하며 단어를 쓰세요. 🎧 MP3-52

first first first first

첫 번째

second second second

두 번째

third third third third

세 번째

fourth fourth fourth fourth

네 번째

fifth fifth fifth fifth

다섯 번째

sixth sixth sixth sixth

여섯 번째

seventh seventh seventh

일곱 번째

eighth eighth eighth eighth

여덟 번째

ninth ninth ninth ninth

아홉 번째

tenth tenth tenth tenth

열 번째

 그림에 맞는 단어를 완성하세요.

❶

eigh◻◻

❷

nin◻◻

❸

ten◻◻

🌷 녹음을 따라 말하며 단어를 쓰세요.   🎧 MP3-53

cake cake cake cake

케이크

candle candle candle candle

양초

gift gift gift gift

선물

age age age age

나이

invite invite invite invite

초대하다

visit visit visit visit

방문하다

bring bring bring bring

가져오다

surprise surprise surprise

놀라게 하다

celebrate celebrate celebrate

축하하다

laugh laugh laugh laugh

웃다

 그림에 맞는 단어를 완성하세요.

❶

c **ke**

❷

v **sit**

❸

lau

월   일
오전   :
오후

 녹음을 따라 말하며 단어를 쓰세요. 🎧 MP3-54

early early early early

이른

late late late late

늦은

noon noon noon noon

정오

tonight tonight tonight

오늘밤

today today today today

오늘

tomorrow tomorrow

내일

 **yesterday** yesterday

어제

 **past** past past past

과거

 **present** present present

현재

 **future** future future future

미래

 그림에 맞는 단어를 완성하세요.

❶

l ⬜ te

❷

tod ⬜ ⬜

❸

⬜ ast

 녹음을 따라 말하며 단어를 쓰세요. 🎧 MP3-55

더운

hot hot hot hot

추운

cold cold cold cold

따뜻한

warm warm warm warm

시원한

cool cool cool cool

화창한

sunny sunny sunny sunny

구름 낀

cloudy cloudy cloudy cloudy

foggy foggy foggy foggy

안개 낀

windy windy windy windy

바람 부는

rainy rainy rainy rainy

비 오는

snowy snowy snowy snowy

눈 오는

 그림에 맞는 단어를 완성하세요.

❶

w ☐ ☐ **m**

❷

sun ☐ ☐

❸

fog ☐ ☐

1. 녹음을 듣고 그림에 맞는 단어를 고르세요. 🎧 MP3-review 11-1

❶

left | right

❷

up | down

❸

south | north

❹

hot | cold

❺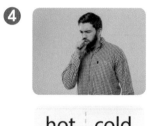

cloudy | windy

❻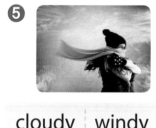

rainy | snowy

2. 녹음을 듣고 단어를 완성하세요. 🎧 MP3-review 11-2

❶   ird   ❷ four   ❸ f th

❹ s th   ❺ gi   ❻ n n

❼   sterday   ❽ pres t   ❾ fu re

3. 단어에 맞는 뜻을 골라 줄로 이으세요.

4. 그림을 보고 퍼즐의 단어를 완성하세요.

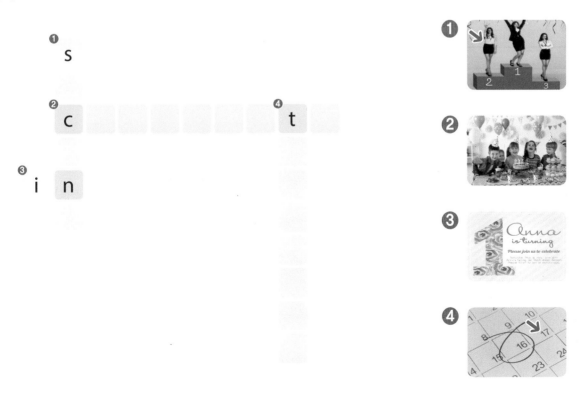

월　　　일
오전
오후　　：

 녹음을 따라 말하며 단어를 쓰세요. 🎧 MP3-56

큰(크다)

big big big big

작은

small small small small

긴(길다)

long long long long

short short short short

짧은

넓은

wide wide wide wide

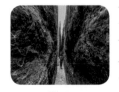

좁은

narrow narrow narrow

same same same same

같은

oval oval oval oval

타원형

rectangle rectangle rectangle

직사각형

cylinder cylinder cylinder

원기둥

 그림에 맞는 단어를 완성하세요.

❶

❷

❸

s me

al

linder

 녹음을 따라 말하며 단어를 쓰세요.　🎧 MP3-57

sick sick sick sick

아프다

hurt hurt hurt hurt

다치게 하다

fever fever fever fever

열나다

cough cough cough cough

기침하다

chest chest chest chest

가슴

stomach stomach stomach

배, 위

heart heart heart heart

심장

medicine medicine medicine

약

life life life life

생명

die die die die

죽다

 그림에 맞는 단어를 완성하세요.

❶

☐☐ ver

❷

☐☐ est

❸

h ☐☐ rt

 녹음을 따라 말하며 단어를 쓰세요. 🎧 MP3-58

gym gym gym gym

체육관

jump rope jump rope

줄넘기

ready ready ready ready

준비하다

turn turn turn turn

돌다

push push push push

밀다

pull pull pull pull

당기다

wrist wrist wrist wrist

손목

elbow elbow elbow elbow

팔꿈치

ankle ankle ankle ankle

발목

waist waist waist waist

허리

 그림에 맞는 단어를 완성하세요.

jump ☐ ☐ **pe**　　　☐ ☐ **ist**　　　☐ ☐ **kle**

월 일
오전 :
오후

 녹음을 따라 말하며 단어를 쓰세요. 🎧 MP3-59

모두

all all all all

거의

most most most most

많은

many many many many

많지 않은

few few few few

많은

much much much much

작은, 약간

little little little little

절반

half half half half

충분한

enough enough enough

텅 빈

empty empty empty empty

채우다

fill fill fill fill

 그림에 맞는 단어를 완성하세요.

❶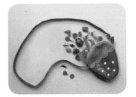

m st

❷

f

❸

enou

DAY 60 Frequency

 녹음을 따라 말하며 단어를 쓰세요. MP3-60

always always always

항상

usually usually usually

대개

often often often often

종종

sometimes sometimes

가끔

who who who who

누구

when when when when

언제

154

where where where where

어디

what what what what

무엇

how how how how

어떻게

why why why why

왜

 그림에 맞는 단어를 완성하세요.

1

al ys

2

us lly

3

o en

1. 녹음을 듣고 그림에 맞는 단어를 고르세요. 🎧 MP3-review 12-1

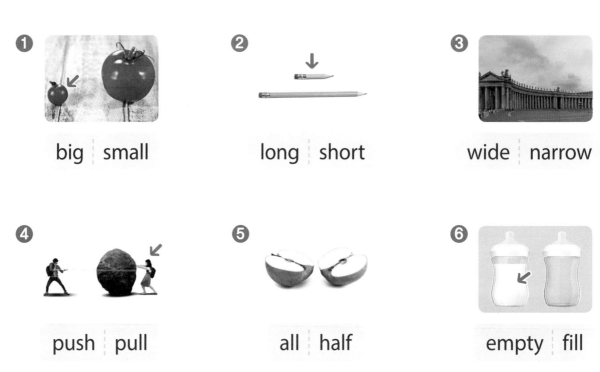

❶ big ┊ small

❷ long ┊ short

❸ wide ┊ narrow

❹ push ┊ pull

❺ all ┊ half

❻ empty ┊ fill

2. 녹음을 듣고 단어를 완성하세요. 🎧 MP3-review 12-2

❶ h　t　❷ r　dy　❸ l　ttle

❹ wh　❺ wh　n　❻ 　ere

❼ w　t　❽ ho　❾ wh

3. 단어에 맞는 뜻을 골라 줄로 이으세요.

❶ sick

• 아프다 •

❷ gym

• 많은 •

❸ elbow

• 팔꿈치 •

❹ many

• 체육관 •

4. 그림을 보고 퍼즐의 단어를 완성하세요.

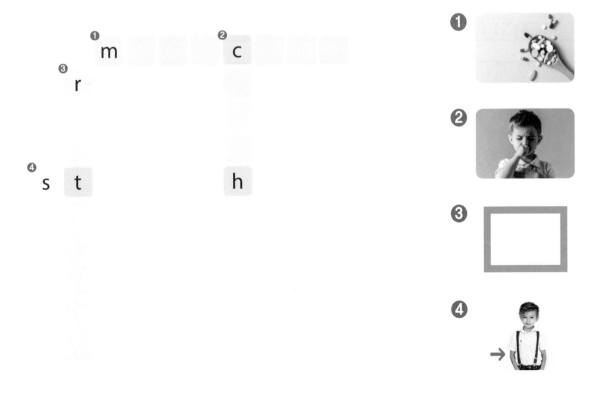

❶ m

❷ c

❸ r

❹ s t   h

정답

DAY 01 ❶ he ❷ she ❸ they

DAY 02 ❶ parents ❷ aunt ❸ uncle

DAY 03 ❶ Bye. ❷ Good morning. ❸ Okay.

DAY 04 ❶ four ❷ seven ❸ eight

DAY 05 ❶ tooth ❷ cheek ❸ chin

REVIEW 01

1. ❶ father ❷ brother ❸ grandmother ❹ two ❺ six ❻ ten

2. ❶ Hi. ❷ lip ❸ eyebrow ❹ you ❺ this ❻ that ❼ everyone ❽ Good afternoon. ❾ You're welcome.

3.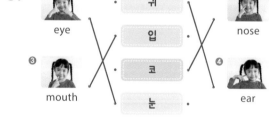

4.
```
        ²n
 ¹e v e n i n g
        g
  ³f ⁴o r e h e a d
    n       t
    e
```

DAY REVIEW

DAY 06 ❶ hair ❷ neck ❸ leg

DAY 07 ❶ skirt ❷ dress ❸ jeans

DAY 08 ❶ door ❷ room ❸ wall

DAY 09 ❶ dog ❷ snake ❸ iguana

DAY 10 ❶ tiger ❷ wolf ❸ pig

REVIEW 02

1. ❶ bedroom ❷ bathroom ❸ window ❹ rabbit ❺ bird ❻ fish

2. ❶ finger ❷ shirt ❸ jacket ❹ elevator ❺ turtle ❻ bear ❼ cow ❽ horse ❾ duck

3.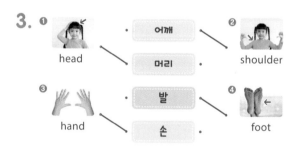

4.
```
          ²s
   ¹g l o v e ⁴s
          c   h
          k   o
  ³p a n t s   e
              s
```

DAY REVIEW

DAY 11 ❶ bread ❷ tea ❸ milk

DAY 12 ❶ apple ❷ kiwi ❸ cherry

DAY 13 ❶ cabbage ❷ sweet potato ❸ chili

DAY 14 ❶ rose ❷ lily ❸ cosmos

DAY 15 ❶ purple ❷ black ❸ white

DAY REVIEW

DAY 16 ❶ guitar ❷ violin ❸ flute

DAY 17 ❶ bat ❷ book ❸ glasses

DAY 18 ❶ car ❷ subway ❸ bicycle

DAY 19 ❶ sad ❷ love ❸ hate

DAY 20 ❶ sit ❷ open ❸ close

REVIEW 03

1. ❶ onion ❷ pumpkin ❸ bean
   ❹ red ❺ green ❻ pink

2. ❶ rice ❷ sandwich ❸ cheese
   ❹ butter ❺ juice ❻ water
   ❼ peach ❽ leaf ❾ pear

3.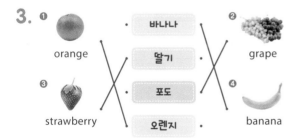

4.
```
 m         s
 o       ² t u l i p
 r         u
 n         f
 i         l
 c a r n a t i o n
   r       w
   g       e
   l       r
   o
   r
   y
```

REVIEW 04

1. ❶ triangle ❷ ball ❸ toy
   ❹ train ❺ truck ❻ airplane

2. ❶ happy ❷ surprised ❸ tired
   ❹ angry ❺ bored ❻ excited
   ❼ come ❽ meet ❾ like

3.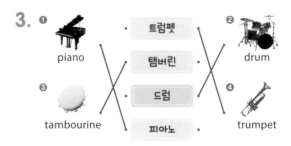

4.
```
      ² u
¹ c o m p u t e r   ³ m
      b           o
      r           t
      e           o
 ⁴ h e l i c o p t e r
      l           c
      a           y
                  c
                  l
                  e
```

정답

DAY REVIEW

DAY 21 ❶ baby ❷ lady ❸ people

DAY 22 ❶ shorts ❷ belt ❸ cap

DAY 23 ❶ eighteen ❷ nineteen
❸ twenty

DAY 24 ❶ sofa ❷ table ❸ bed

DAY 25 ❶ shower ❷ soap ❸ stove

DAY REVIEW

DAY 26 ❶ delicious ❷ sweet ❸ bitter

DAY 27 ❶ gorilla ❷ panda ❸ deer

DAY 28 ❶ whale ❷ octopus
❸ shrimp

DAY 29 ❶ brush ❷ paint ❸ make

DAY 30 ❶ picture ❷ photo ❸ fan

REVIEW 05

1. ❶ girl ❷ man ❸ television
❹ twelve ❺ fifteen ❻ pillow

2. ❶ button ❷ pocket ❸ sweater
❹ boots ❺ bathtub ❻ toilet
❼ shampoo ❽ chopsticks ❾ closet

3.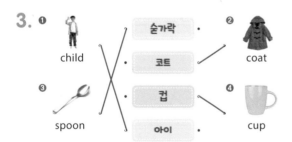

child · 숟가락 · coat
· 코트 ·
· 컵 ·
spoon · 아이 · cup

4.
```
        r
    g   e
h a n d k e r c h i e f
    t   i
    l   g
    e   e
    m   c u r t a i n
    a   a
    n   t
        o
        r
```

REVIEW 06

1. ❶ egg ❷ giraffe ❸ starfish
❹ circle ❺ square ❻ lamp

2. ❶ eat ❷ drink ❸ monkey
❹ shark ❺ squid ❻ vase
❼ album ❽ cut ❾ key

3.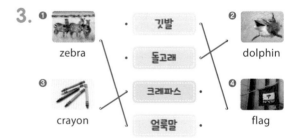

zebra · 깃발 · dolphin
· 돌고래 ·
· 크레파스 ·
crayon · 얼룩말 · flag

4.
```
b r e a k f a s t
          a
        p e n g u i n
          g
          a
    o s t r i c h
          o
          o
```

DAY REVIEW

DAY 31 ❶ month ❷ year ❸ date

DAY 32 ❶ August ❷ September
❸ October

DAY 33 ❶ holiday ❷ vacation
❸ Christmas

DAY 34 ❶ sky ❷ land ❸ thunder

DAY 35 ❶ soccer ❷ baseball ❸ skate

DAY REVIEW

DAY 36 ❶ cooking ❷ draw ❸ travel

DAY 37 ❶ nurse ❷ scientist
❸ musician

DAY 38 ❶ new ❷ tall ❸ pretty

DAY 39 ❶ great ❷ upset ❸ sleepy

DAY 40 ❶ start ❷ walk ❸ ride

REVIEW 07

1. ❶ week ❷ December ❸ star
   ❹ January ❺ April ❻ June

2. ❶ second ❷ minute ❸ hour
   ❹ sea ❺ river ❻ sun
   ❼ rainbow ❽ volleyball ❾ tennis

3.
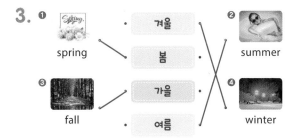

❶ spring — 봄
❷ summer — 여름
❸ fall — 가을
❹ winter — 겨울

4.
```
      ¹t
       a
       b
  ²c a l e n d a r
       e
       t
³b a s k e t b a l l
       n
       n
⁴b o w l i n g
       s
```

REVIEW 08

1. ❶ sing ❷ kite ❸ artist
   ❹ heavy ❺ scared ❻ full

2. ❶ movie ❷ ugly ❸ dark
   ❹ fall ❺ help ❻ finish
   ❼ move ❽ continue ❾ call

3.
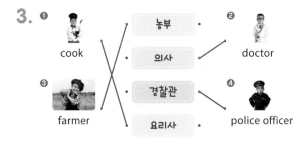

❶ cook — 요리사
❷ doctor — 의사
❸ farmer — 농부
❹ police officer — 경찰관

4.
```
              ⁴t
         ³c    h
¹→²b e a u t i f u l
   r    m    r
   i    e    s
   g    r    t
   h    a    y
   t
```

DAY REVIEW

DAY 41 ❶ Korea ❷ China ❸ America
DAY 42 ❶ bakery ❷ library ❸ theater
DAY 43 ❶ desk ❷ chair ❸ bag
DAY 44 ❶ slide ❷ hide ❸ find
DAY 45 ❶ picnic ❷ run ❸ smile

DAY REVIEW

DAY 46 ❶ soup ❷ beef ❸ bowl
DAY 47 ❶ groceries ❷ snack
　　　　　 ❸ beverage
DAY 48 ❶ forest ❷ lake ❸ rock
DAY 49 ❶ hat ❷ sunglasses ❸ bottle
DAY 50 ❶ middle ❷ corner ❸ end

REVIEW 09

1. ❶ hospital ❷ bank ❸ bench
　 ❹ jump ❺ kick ❻ pencil

2. ❶ world ❷ Japan ❸ Canada
　 ❹ England ❺ France ❻ textbook
　 ❼ catch ❽ field ❾ relax

3.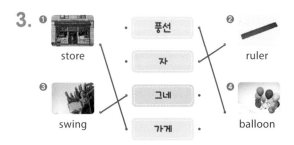
　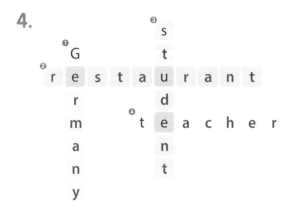

store ── 가게
풍선
자
그네
ruler
balloon
swing

4.
```
        ³s
   ¹G   t
²r e s t a u r a n t
   r    d
   m  ⁴t e a c h e r
   a    n
   n    t
   y
```

REVIEW 10

1. ❶ sugar ❷ tree ❸ top
　 ❹ buy ❺ expensive ❻ behind

2. ❶ hill ❷ pond ❸ ocean
　 ❹ wave ❺ sand ❻ swim
　 ❼ here ❽ there ❾ break

3.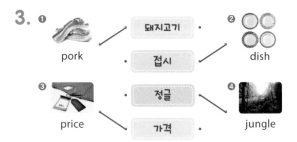

pork ── 돼지고기
접시 ── dish
price ── 가격
정글 ── jungle

4.
```
¹s u n ²s c r e e n
        h
      ³c l i m b
        c
        k
      ⁴p e p p e r
        n
```

DAY REVIEW

DAY 51 ❶ east ❷ west ❸ straight
DAY 52 ❶ eighth ❷ ninth ❸ tenth
DAY 53 ❶ cake ❷ visit ❸ laugh
DAY 54 ❶ late ❷ today ❸ past
DAY 55 ❶ warm ❷ sunny ❸ foggy

DAY REVIEW

DAY 56 ❶ same ❷ oval ❸ cylinder
DAY 57 ❶ fever ❷ chest ❸ heart
DAY 58 ❶ jump rope ❷ wrist ❸ ankle
DAY 59 ❶ most ❷ few ❸ enough
DAY 60 ❶ always ❷ usually ❸ often

REVIEW 11

1. ❶ left ❷ down ❸ south
   ❹ cold ❺ windy ❻ snowy

2. ❶ third ❷ fourth ❸ fifth
   ❹ sixth ❺ gift ❻ noon
   ❼ yesterday ❽ present ❾ future

3.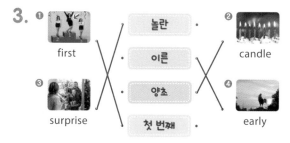
first
surprise
놀란
이른
양초
첫 번째
candle
early

4.
```
      ❶
       s
      ❷
       c e l e b r a t e
   ❸     o          m
       i n v i t e    o
         d            r
                      r
                      o
                      w
```

REVIEW 12

1. ❶ small ❷ short ❸ wide
   ❹ push ❺ half ❻ fill

2. ❶ hurt ❷ ready ❸ little
   ❹ who ❺ when ❻ where
   ❼ what ❽ how ❾ why

3.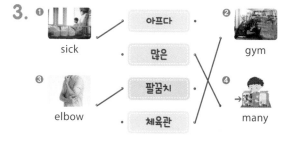
sick
elbow
아프다
많은
팔꿈치
체육관
gym
many

4.
```
        ❶          ❷
         m e d i c i n e
      ❸  r          o
         e          u
         c          g
      ❹  s t o m a c h
         a
         n
         g
         l
         e
```

찾아보기

C

찾아보기

S

가장 쉬운
초등영단어 따라쓰기 하루 한 장의 기적

초판 6쇄 2022년 12월 5일 | **저자** 동양북스 콘텐츠기획팀 | **발행인** 김태웅 | **마케팅** 나재승 | **제작** 현대순 | **기획 편집** 양정화 | **디자인** 남은혜, 신효선

발행처 (주)동양북스 | **등록** 제2014-000055호(2014년 2월 7일) | **주소** 서울시 마포구 동교로 22길14 (04030) | **구입문의** | 전화 (02)337-1737 **팩스** (02)334-6624

내용문의 | 전화 (02)337-1763 dybooks2@gmail.com

ISBN 979-11-5768-427-4 63740

▶ 본 책은 저작권법에 의해 보호를 받는 저작물이므로 무단 전재와 복제를 금합니다.
▶ 잘못된 책은 구입처에서 교환해드립니다.
▶ 도서출판 동양북스에서는 소중한 원고, 새로운 기획을 기다리고 있습니다.
  http://www.dongyangbooks.com